Forms of Energy

Herbert West

The Rosen Publishing Group's

PowerKids Press™

New York

Published in 2009 by The Rosen Publishing Group, Inc.
29 East 21st Street, New York, NY 10010

Copyright © 2009 by The Rosen Publishing Group, Inc.

Book Design: Michael J. Flynn

Photo Credits: Cover, p. 13 (wind turbine) © absolut/Shutterstock; p. 3 © sn4ke/Shutterstock; p. 5 © Toru Yamanaka/AFP/Getty Images; p. 6 © Katrina Leigh/Shutterstock; p. 7 (baseball players) © Chad McDermott/Shutterstock; p. 7 (book) © Vladimir Melnikov/Shutterstock; p. 7 (desk) © 7505811966/Shutterstock; p. 8 © Todd Taulman/Shutterstock; p. 9 © Slavoljub Pantelic/Shutterstock; p. 10 (toaster) © Les Scholz/Shutterstock; p. 10 (lightbulb) © Igor Smichkov/Shutterstock; p. 10 (lightning) © Shane Thomas Shaw/Shutterstock; p. 12 (fan) © Osvaldru/Shutterstock; p. 12 (electric motor) © Yury Kosourov/Shutterstock; p. 13 (generator) © Bestweb/Shutterstock; p. 14 © Nadiya/Shutterstock; p. 16 © Jonathan Brizendine/Shutterstock; p. 17 © Noah Golan/Shutterstock; p. 18 (trombone player) © Johannes Compaan/Shutterstock; p. 18 (train) © Chris H. Galbraith/Shutterstock; p. 19 © Ken Hurst/Shutterstock; p. 20 (molecule) © Stephen Sweet/Shutterstock; p. 21 (power plant) © Petr Nad/Shutterstock; p. 22 © Elena Ray/Shutterstock.

Library of Congress Cataloging-in-Publication Data

West, Herbert.
  Forms of energy / Herbert West.
    p. cm. — (Real life readers)
  Includes index.
  ISBN: 978-1-4358-0123-3
  6-pack ISBN: 978-1-4358-0124-0
  ISBN 978-1-4358-2975-6 (library binding)
  1. Force and energy—Juvenile literature. 2. Power (Mechanics)—Juvenile literature. I. Title.
  QC73.4.W457 2009
  531'.6—dc22

                              2008036802

Manufactured in the United States of America

Contents

What Is Energy?

Do you like roller coasters? Have you ever wondered what makes a roller coaster climb to the top of the first hill and race down the other side?

The answer is energy. Energy is the ability to make change and do work. We use energy every day to do many things, not only to move roller coasters. We use energy to ride a bike and power a car. We use energy to heat our homes and cook dinner. There are many ways to produce energy, such as using your muscles or starting a fire. We can use up a **source** of energy, or we can store energy to use at a later time. Some sources of energy will last forever. Even **gravity** can be a source of energy.

There are many different kinds of energy. How many can you think of?

Many roller coasters use a motor and a long chain to get the cars to the top of the first hill. Once they are there, the force of gravity pulls the cars back down the hill.

What is it?
The ability to make change and do work

about energy sources
- we can use up some sources
- we can save some sources for later
- some sources will last forever

Energy

examples
- using our muscles to move a bike
- using gas to power a car
- using a motor and chain to move a roller coaster

not examples
- bike
- car
- roller coaster

5

Energy at Rest and in Motion

The most basic form of energy is **mechanical** energy. There are two kinds of mechanical energy. Potential, or stored, energy is the

energy an object has because of its position. A yo-yo with its string wound up has potential energy. Water held back by a dam has potential energy. These objects have stored energy that can be set free under the right conditions.

Kinetic energy is the energy an object has because of its motion. Gravity is a source of kinetic energy because it makes things fall to Earth. The more mass and speed an object has, the greater its kinetic energy is. A car traveling 55 miles per hour (89 kph) has more kinetic energy than a baseball traveling at the same speed because it's heavier. However, a thrown baseball has greater kinetic energy than a car at rest.

A book on a desk has potential energy because of its position high above the ground. If someone knocks the book off the desk, the potential energy changes into kinetic energy as gravity pulls the book to the ground.

7

Energy is often thought of as the ability to do work. Mechanical energy has the ability to move an object by applying force to it. A raised hammer, for example, has potential energy. This means that it has stored energy and is ready to do work. When the hammer is swung toward a nail in a block of wood, the potential energy changes into kinetic energy. The kinetic energy allows the hammer to apply force to the nail. The force displaces, or moves, the nail and drives it into the wood. The hammer regains potential energy after it has been raised for another swing.

Energy can't be created or destroyed. It can, however, change forms. All forms of energy can be sorted as kinetic or potential.

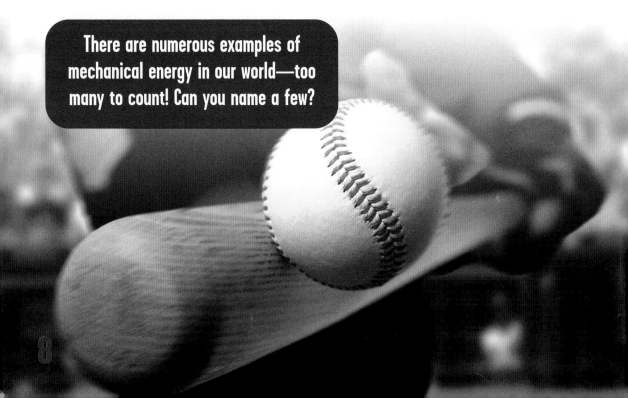

There are numerous examples of mechanical energy in our world—too many to count! Can you name a few?

Mechanical Energy

potential

stored energy

Examples
- wound-up yo-yo
- water behind a dam
- book on a desk
- raised hammer

kinetic

energy in motion

Examples
- moving car
- thrown ball
- falling book
- moving hammer

10

Electricity and Magnets

What do you think of when you hear the word "energy"? Many people think of electricity because it's the type of energy that we most commonly use in our homes, schools, and offices. Electricity is used to power lights, TVs, computers, and many other things. Without electricity, our world would be a very different place.

Electricity is a form of kinetic energy. It's the movement of very tiny **particles** called electrons. Electrons are one type of matter that make up atoms, which are the tiny bits of matter that make up everything around us. Electrons are often able to flow from one atom to another. When this happens along a wire, electricity is made.

Lightning is a form of electricity. Electrons build up in the bottoms of clouds before a storm. When enough build up, they race downward. This causes other particles to race up from the ground, which causes a bolt of lightning.

11

Magnetism is a type of force commonly used in our world. In fact, Earth itself is one huge magnet! All magnets, even Earth, create a force around them that pushes and pulls some types of matter, particularly iron. This is called a magnetic field.

Did you know that electricity and magnetic force are very closely related? A magnetic field is created by the movement of electrons. Magnets work because they have groups of atoms whose electrons all move in the same direction. When many of these groups line up and point in the same direction, the object they make up becomes a magnet. Magnetic force surrounds and is created by an electrical current. Magnetic force can also be used to make an electrical current.

electric motor

generator

An electric motor, such as the one used in an electric fan, uses magnets to change electricity into movement. A generator, such as the one used in a modern windmill, uses magnets to change movement into electricity.

Light and Heat

Light is called electromagnetic (EM) energy because it's made up of waves of electricity and waves of magnetic force. Other forms of EM energy include X-rays and radio waves. Light is the only form of EM energy that we can see without special instruments. EM energy is kinetic energy. It never stops moving once it's produced, as long as nothing gets in its way.

Light is the energy that allows us to see the world around us. It's made up of different-sized waves that create all the colors we see. When light hits an object, some of the waves are **reflected** and some are **absorbed**. We see the waves that are reflected. When light hits grass, for example, the grass absorbs all colors except green. Green light waves are reflected. That's why grass looks green.

The range of colors people are able to see is called the spectrum. We can see the spectrum in a rainbow.

Heat, a form of kinetic energy, is produced by the movement of the atoms that make up matter. It may also result from other forms of energy at work within a system or object. When electricity flows through a wire, for example, the wire may get hot because of the movement of electrons. Heat naturally moves from a hot area to a colder area.

Most toasters have wires that heat up when electricity flows through them. The wires are hot enough to toast bread.

Heat and light often go hand in hand. When most objects absorb light, the energy is changed into heat. A heated object, such as wood, may glow or burn and make light. Our greatest source of heat and light is the sun. Without it, we would not be able to live. For millions of years, the sun has kept animals warm and helped plants make food. Energy from the sun is called solar energy.

16

These are solar panels. They're used to change solar energy into electricity.

We can hear the sounds of our world because the space around us is filled with air, which is a medium for sound waves.

Sound

Did you know that sound is a form of kinetic energy, too? Sound, like light, travels in waves. Sound waves can travel through all kinds of matter, including solids, liquids, and gases. The matter through which sound waves travel is called the **medium**. Sound can't travel when there is no medium. For example, sound can't travel in outer space because there's no matter. Sound waves cause matter to **vibrate**, or move up and down and back and forth very quickly. This allows the sound wave to travel through the medium.

Changes in the height and length of sound waves cause different sounds. Some sounds are too high for people to hear, and some are too low.

19

Chemical and Nuclear Energy

Chemical energy is potential energy stored in the bonds that hold atoms and **molecules** together. When these bonds break, the chemical energy can move to another molecule or atom, or it can be released in another form. For example, burning coal or oil breaks the bonds between their molecules and releases energy in the form of light and heat.

model of a molecule

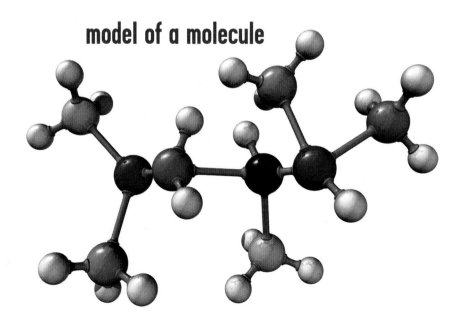

Nuclear energy is another type of potential energy. It's the energy that holds an atom's nucleus, or center, together. It can be released by breaking the nucleus of an atom apart. It can also be released by combining the centers of atoms. This is how the sun makes heat and light.

Some power plants use nuclear energy to make electricity. This is a picture of nuclear power plant.

We use the forms of energy discussed in this book for many purposes. The table below shows examples of each form of energy. Do you know any others?

form of energy	potential	kinetic	example
mechanical	X	X	power a bike using your muscles
electricity		X	power the computer in your home
light		X	light a dark street so it is safe to drive on
heat		X	cook food
sound		X	**sonar** uses sound waves to see the ocean floor
chemical	X		gas in a car burns and releases energy
nuclear	X		used to power some spaceships

Glossary

absorb (uhb-SORB) To take in and hold on to something.

gravity (GRA-vuh-tee) The natural force that causes objects to move toward the center of Earth.

mechanical (mih-KA-nih-kuhl) Having to do with the effects of forces on objects.

medium (MEE-dee-uhm) Matter through which something passes.

molecule (MAH-lih-kyool) Two or more atoms joined together.

particle (PAHR-tih-kuhl) A very tiny piece of matter.

reflect (rih-FLEKT) To throw back light, heat, or sound.

sonar (SOH-nahr) An instrument that locates things by sending out sound waves and measuring how long it takes for the reflected sound to come back.

source (SOHRS) The place from which something starts.

vibrate (VY-brayt) To move back and forth quickly.

Index

Due to the changing nature of Internet links, The Rosen Publishing Group, Inc., has developed an online list of Web sites related to the subject of this book. This site is updated regularly. Please use this link to access the list: http://www.rcbmlinks.com/rlr/energ